Building a Better Garden: DIY Gardening Projects

Modern Simplicity, Book 6

Anna Hess, Duncan Wall

Contents

Introduction

Hey there, fellow gardeners! Welcome to a world in which your backyard is not only beautiful, but also incredibly productive. The DIY projects that I'll introduce in this book are guaranteed to make your garden the envy of the neighborhood.

Imagine your very own backyard oasis brimming with bug-free greens and luscious fruits, all achieved through ingenious techniques that shield your precious crops and squeeze every last drop of potential out of your space. Whether you're a beginner dreaming of growing your own food or a seasoned pro looking to sprinkle some new magic into your plot of earth, these hands-on projects are tailor-made for you.

We'll start by growing flourishing gardens right on your porch with stylish yet functional planter boxes that will both nurture your plants and make your life a whole lot easier.

Next up are insect pests. Of all the problems out there, these are the ones most likely to tempt even organic gardeners to spray. Why not instead opt for a one-time structural fix that'll keep the bugs permanently at bay?

After that, I'll show you how to build deer-proof fences. If critters have ever treated your garden like an all-you-can-eat buffet, these will have Bambi looking elsewhere for a snack.

Finally, I'll show you the secrets to big berry harvests. Say goodbye to sharing your raspberries with birds and your strawberries with chipmunks!

Are you ready to roll up your sleeves and create a garden that's as impressive as it is delicious? Then keep reading as we dive into these DIY gardening projects.

About the Walden Effect Team

This book started out as a course on Udemy, and it might have stayed that way if we hadn't been fortunate enough to get help.

Luckily, Duncan Wall came on board to turn videos into words on the page and still pictures. He did an amazing job, and any mistakes are definitely not his.

Instead, the buck stops with the core Walden Effect team. I'm Anna Hess, the author of *The Weekend Home-steader* plus a bunch of other books. And my husband, Mark Hamilton, is the inventor of the Avian Aqua Miser, which revolutionized backyard chicken keeping.

When we approach gardening projects, Mark and I come at it from two very different points of view. I like to look at things from the ecosystem perspective, so I'm all about improving the soil and making sure that our plants thrive. Mark instead looks at a gardening problem, pulls out his drill gun, and says, "I can fix that".

In other words, *DIY Gardening Projects* is the result of fifteen years of my honey-do list filtered through Mark's inventive streak. His constructions solved my gardening problems, and I hope that they solve yours too!

Where to Start

This book doesn't have to be read in order. Instead, every chapter is a project that can stand entirely on its own. The summary below might help guide you toward the best project to start with, or you can just turn the page and dive right in.

Porch Planter Boxes:

- Difficulty: Intermediate

- Cost: Moderate

- Primary benefits: Accessible and prime growing space

Anti-Caterpillar Tunnels:

- Difficulty: Intermediate

- Cost: Low

- Primary benefits: Insect protection, season extension

Deer-proof Garden Fence:

- Difficulty: Advanced

- Cost: High

- Primary benefits: Keeps deer out of the garden

Critter-proof Strawberry Beds:

- Difficulty: Intermediate

- Cost: Low

- Primary benefits: Keeps birds and rodents out of low-growing plants

Anti-Bird netting:

- Difficulty: Intermediate

- Cost: Low

- Primary benefits: Keeps birds out of high-growing berry bushes

Plant Support with U-Posts:

- Difficulty: Easy

- Cost: Low

- Primary benefits: Simple plant management

Finally, before you start, I want to point you toward the supply list at the very end of this book. We compiled a rundown of everything you'll need for each project, which should make your shopping a little easier if you decide to give any of these projects a try.

Now get ready to pull out your tools and build a better garden!

Porch Planter Boxes

Why We Love Our Porch Planter Boxes

We're big fans of porch planter boxes for two main reasons:

Prime growing area. First, planter boxes are often better places for plants to take root. In September of 2023, for example, we enjoyed a long-lived cherry tomato exploding out of our planter box while almost all tomato plants in the garden had grown blighted and died. By being up off the ground, mold levels in the planter box stay low. No wonder plants prone to fungal infections tend to thrive there!

Maximum attention. Another great thing about the planter boxes is that they're close to your living area, so the plants get plenty of human attention. One summer in our main garden, the timer in our drip-irrigation system died and I didn't notice for weeks. (Oops.) But Mark drops by his planter boxes two or three times per day, wielding a watering wand when necessary. As the saying goes, a gardener's attention is the best fertilizer.

How to Build a Porch Planter Box

The construction of a porch planter box is pretty straightforward. Start by building a frame out of 2x4s, attaching the frame to nearby building walls (if possible) to add stability. 4x4 posts at each corner and shelf brackets screwed into the porch deck keep the planter box sturdy and anchored. Plywood sides will hold in the soil.

That's all you absolutely need to build a porch planter box, but ours have extra features that come highly recommended:

- **We paint our porch planter boxes.** Not only does this make them look pretty, but it increases their durability. Be sure to use exterior paint — the stuff labeled for barns and fences will work well here.

- **Vinyl siding is a paint alternative.** Adding vinyl siding to the outside of your plywood walls serves the same purpose as paint and will help the planter box blend into nearby structures.

- **One of our porch planter boxes has an herb shelf attached.** All it takes is an extra 2x8 or 2x10 board affixed to the edge of the box, supported by shelf brackets. This shelf is great for holding potted herbs that don't need deep root space, and it can also be used for storing tools or putting down your watering can for a moment. More space is always a plus.

- **Instead of a wall, one side of our smaller box boasts a glass window.** You can often find used windows at reuse stores, where they may be as cheap or sometimes even cheaper than plywood. You'll need to take a bit more care during construction so you don't break the glass. (Been there, done that.) But afterwards, you can see the dirt and root growth through the window. It's fun to observe how far down your plants extend!

Filling Up Your Porch Planter Box

Once you've built your planter box, it's time to fill it up! There are several options to choose from:

- **Potting soil.** This is a high-quality planting medium, but it can get quite expensive.

- **Manure.** The cheapest option and the one we went for... mostly.

- **Compost.** Purchased bulk compost is a good middle ground in terms of price.

- **Mixtures.** If used potting soil is going to waste at the end of the growing season, don't throw it out. Instead, spread the worn-out soil on top of your manure or compost to create an excellent seedbed for next year's crops. The old potting soil will be low in nutrients, but plant roots will soon grow down into the richer area underneath. Worms will mix the layers together over time and the potting soil will improve your soil texture.

The only thing I don't recommend filling your planter box with is dirt dug out of the ground. Unimproved soil tends to be compacted and poorly draining in a container situation. So definitely give that idea a pass.

Another bad idea — but one we swear by — is filling our porch planter boxes most of the way up with fresh manure. As you likely know, planting directly into uncomposted manure is a recipe for dead plants. But we get away with putting fresh horse manure in the bottom of our boxes because we then layer used potting soil on top. By the time our plants grow down to the manure, the heat has cooked out. You may even get a slight "hot box" effect in early spring when the fresh manure helps your seedlings along by warming the soil above.

Once you've chosen your soil type, how do you fill the planter box up? A great way to get manure or compost into your planter box is with a good old 5-gallon bucket. These are easy to move around, but lifting the buckets up into the planter can be quite strenuous for some. If you need to ask for help, this would be the time to hire the neighborhood kid!

Dealing with Roof Runoff

Every porch planter box is different because every porch is different. In our case (and maybe yours?) runoff from a nearby roof became a problem, washing away seedlings and splashing soil out of the planter box.

Mark's solution to the runoff issue was to add clear plastic roofing material over the box. This causes rain to rush past the planter box while still letting sunlight through to nourish the plants underneath. As a bonus, the area under the roof tends to be even more fungus-free than our other planter boxes.

One downside to this approach, however, is that the crops there become 100% dependent on us for water. Plus, turbo-charged plants may want to grow higher than your roof. In the end, it's worth weighing the pros and cons before taking this approach.

What to Grow in Your Porch Planter Box

Now that everything is set up, it's time to decide what to grow in your porch planter box. There are a lot of crops you can try, and also some I recommend skipping in this location.

Luffa is an example of something that grows really well in a porch planter box, but nonetheless, I don't recommend planting it there. At the end of a long growing season, you may end up with only one fruit from the entire plant. The same disadvantage applies to **winter squash, potatoes,** or any other plant that only produces a small number of fruits per season. You're  simply not going to get much bang for your buck.

Other crops in the better-to-skip category include:

- asparagus

- beets

- broccoli

- brussels sprouts

- cabbage

- carrots

- corn

- garlic

- eggplant

- melons

- onions

- peppers

- rhubarb

- sweet potatoes

In contrast, **tomatoes** are a great fit for porch planter boxes, especially cherry tomatoes (also known as tommy toes). Once a tomato plant gets up and running, you'll be able to harvest from it every day for months right on your porch. Convenient and economical! The other really great thing about a cherry tomato plant is that it grows up, rather than out, meaning that it takes up less of your box's limited space. To extend your harvest over time, I also recommend choosing indeterminate varieties of cherry tomatoes.

Other top crops for a porch planter box include:

- cucumbers

- green beans

- lettuce and other leafy greens (although they use up more horizontal space than some of the other options)

- okra (a great fit for areas that need to appear ornamental)

- peas

- radishes

- summer squash

In the fruit department, we're experimenting with a grapevine since it can be trained to shade the rest of the porch and only uses up a little bit of our planter box. Kiwis fit into a similar category if you live in a region warm enough to keep them happy. Most other fruits, though, are going to require lots of space while only producing a crop once per year, meaning they're not a great fit for most planter boxes.

Finally, **herbs** are an excellent crop to keep right outside your door since you're more likely to snip a leaf here or there to season dinner if you don't have to walk far to do so. However, most herbs don't require the deep root area that a planter box provides. Instead, I recommend setting herbs in a pot on the planter box's shelf and saving your planter's valuable space for something else.

Dealing with Shade

One last factor to consider when selecting plants for your planter box is sun. Porches are, by definition, located beside buildings, and those buildings cast shade. For us, the area right up against our house doesn't get enough sun for most vegetables, so we've instead been growing our veggies out further from the wall. It's possible, however, to use the shadier areas of your box to grow cool-season crops, especially lettuce, during the summer months. It might also be worth it to "waste" this space on herbs.

Another option is to mitigate the shade issue using trellises, which can be built out of wire or lumber. By training your plants to grow up instead of out, trellises maximize your porch planter box's space and help crops move up into the sun.

Season Extension in the Planter Box

If you want to start growing in the very early spring, there's a super simple addition you can place onto your porch planter box to protect your crops from frost. All you need to do is create a frame out of furring strips or other thin pieces of lumber, making sure it fits well atop your planter box. Then screw on some Agribon fabric, which I'll talk about in the next chapter. This is a great way to give early spring crops a jump start on the year.

Annual Maintenance

I'll end this chapter with the tasks you'll want to complete each year to make sure your porch planter box continues giving you a great crop.

- **Rake away the dead stalks of last year's plants.** Removing spent growth makes room for new plants, and removing diseased tops prevents contamination of next year's crop.

- **Top off the box with more potting soil, compost, and/or manure.** Over the course of a growing season, the contents will slowly settle. Plus, you'll need more nutrients for the next season's growth.

Otherwise, growing in a planter box is just like growing in the ground ... only your yields will be higher and you'll enjoy the greenery each time you open your door. Enjoy the bountiful harvests from your porch planter box!

(Anti-)Caterpillar Tunnels

Why We Love Our Caterpillar Tunnels

Anyone who's grown crucifers in an organic manner can tell you that the biggest problem is cabbage worms.

These guys look really cute and fuzzy. But for creatures that are so small, they pose a big problem. Certain crucifers like broccoli or brussels sprouts need to grow for several months in the summer when freezes won't kill the surrounding insect life. Unfortunately, if you leave those plants out in the open without spraying insecticides or hand-squishing the bugs, the cabbage worms are going to eat your entire crop.

I used to come out to my broccoli plants every other day and murder the cute little cabbage worms. The task wasn't entirely pleasant, and it wasn't entirely effective either. Can you even see the cabbage worm in the photo to the right? Suffice it to say, I missed a lot.

When Mark saw me in action, he exclaimed, "It's time to work smart, not hard!" The result was our beloved caterpillar tunnels.

I'll show you how to build your own caterpillar tunnels in the next section. But while I'm still trying to sell you on the effort, here are some additional advantages to consider:

- The tunnels are extremely easy to open, so you can get in there to weed and harvest without much effort.

- When they're closed up, the anti-insect netting on the tunnels keeps out the egg-laying butterflies and moths that give rise to cabbage worms. It also blocks out squash bugs, flea beetles, and larger critters like rabbits and groundhogs.

- Meanwhile, sunlight, air and water easily pass through the netting. This means you don't have to do anything special with the plants under these structures, which is a major plus.

Starting Seeds Under Caterpillar Tunnels

Although their primary use is to keep out insects that nibble on plants, caterpillar tunnels also turn out to aid germination for tricky crops.

Anyone who's grown carrots knows that getting seeds to sprout is often the most difficult step. Carrot seeds take a long time to emerge, and you often broadcast them at times of the year when the soil isn't at an optimum moisture level for germination. The result is spotty sprouting, with just enough carrots coming up so you can't use the bed for anything else but not really enough to make the crop worth your while.

However, I've found that germina-tion increases when I cover my newly planted carrot beds with caterpillar tunnels. (In the photo to the right, the half of the bed on the right was under a caterpillar tunnel; the half on the left wasn't.) I can't tell you exactly  why this happens, but my best guess is that the caterpillar tunnels provide a slightly warmer microclimate in early spring, and the ground might also be a little moister under cover. Whatever the reason, germination is definitely improved beneath caterpillar tunnels.

I also often start peas and beans under caterpillar tunnels, not to promote germination but to decrease nibbling. Unfortunately, rabbits find it easy to wiggle through our fence, and they love pea and bean sprouts. Covering up those beds up for a few weeks is all it takes to get the legumes off to a good start without providing a buffet for local wildlife.

Finally, caterpillar tunnels are great for jump-starting cucurbits, a family of plants that include squashes, cucumbers and melons. In this case, my issues with direct seeding into the garden have to do with the tender plants getting eaten up by bugs before they have time to produce any fruit. However, if you put cucurbit plantings under a caterpillar tunnel for the first month or so of their life, the seedlings will grow past the delicious stage unscathed. Of course, unlike with crucifers, you'll need to remove the tunnel at bloom time since cucurbits won't get pollinated by the good bugs while living undercover.

In short, caterpillar tunnels are great for growing many crops that don't do so well when directly seeded into the garden without extra care. No wonder I'm constantly in need of more caterpillar tunnels!

How to Build a Caterpillar Tunnel

Are you sold? If so, your first step is to decide between the tried-and-true Version 1.0 or the experimental Version 2.0.

Version 1.0

For our oldest caterpillar tunnels, Mark started by building a frame out of 2x3s, choosing those over the more widely available 2x4s because they're a little lighter. I frequently move our tunnels around the garden by myself, so it's important for them not to be too heavy. However, the tunnels we made with painted 2x3s are starting to rot out after only about three years, while 2x4s would have lasted longer. In the end, the type of lumber you decide to build your caterpillar tunnels with is up to you.

Regardless of whether you use 2x3s or 2x4s, make a rectangle out of your wood. A good use of lumber is a rectangle 8 ft. by 4 ft. or 4 ft. by 4 ft. The latter requires more materials per square foot and twice as much work to assemble, but the smaller option is really easy for one person to move and gives you more options for arranging them in your garden.

Either way, create a second rectangle of the same size to go on top of the first one. Then hinge the two rectangles together on the back with door hinges. (Remember: we include links to recommended products in the Supply List!)

After that, add the hoops onto your frame. Mark used 1/2-inch PVC pipes bent into a hoop shape for our Version 1.0 tunnels, inserting each end into a hole drilled into the top piece of the frame using a 7/8-inch hole saw and bored out a little bit more with a 3/4-inch spade bit. He didn't drill straight down, considering instead the angle at which the bent pipe would contact the frame. Working with this inclination rather than correcting it makes construction considerably easier. A note on longevity, however: these holes do become a weak point after a few years.

Our Version 1.0 caterpillar tunnel is eight feet long to optimize the framing lumber. For this size, five hoops works really well. You can scale that to your own caterpillar tunnel as appropriate — I especially like four-foot tunnels that use three hoops apiece.

Running across the top of the hoops, Mark added a furring strip to connect all of the hoops together and give them a little more stability. To connect this top piece, he simply wired it onto both ends of the structure. If you're building a shorter tunnel, you don't really need the extra stability, so you can skip this step. Either way, now's a good time to paint any exposed wood.

Next, choose insect-barrier fabric to lay over the top of the hoops. When we first built our caterpillar tunnels, I used wedding-tulle fabric on the recommendation of various internet forums, but the result didn't last even one season before the barrier was peppered with holes. After that experience, we paid the extra money for professional-grade insect-barrier fabric, which is still working well after four years. For us, longevity is definitely worth the additional cost.

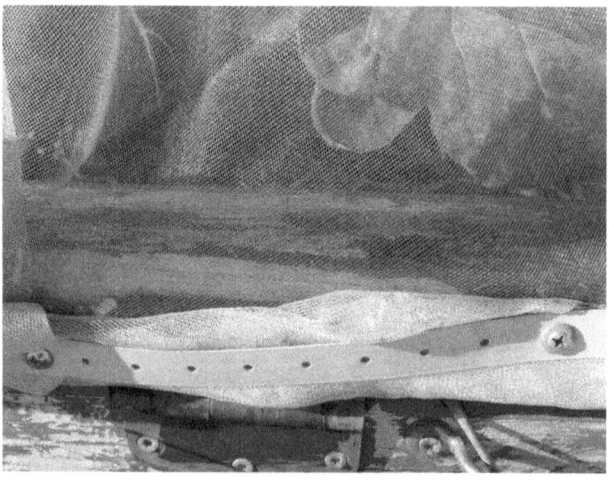

Whatever fabric you choose, cut it to size by laying it over the caterpillar-tunnel frame, being sure the fabric reaches the ground on all sides. To attach the fabric to the tunnel, our first attempt involved rolling the ends of the fabric up a few times, then screwing lag screws through a sandwich consisting of plastic strapping, the fabric, and the framing wood. In a later section, I'll tell you about a new experimental method for attaching the fabric that Mark likes better, but this method works okay.

Mark also added a support strap to our Version 1.0 model, which holds the caterpillar tunnel open while I'm working inside. One end of the strap is screwed to the front of the bottom frame, and the other to the front of the top frame. It's a balancing act to make the strap long enough to keep the lid from falling closed on the gardener's head but short enough not to crush the plants in the next row over. You'll need to experiment to get it right.

A facet of the Version 1.0 tunnel that I'm less keen on is the inclusion of carrying handles. Personally, I tend to just lift up the tunnel and put it on my shoulders when moving it, rendering these handles useless in my garden. They might be more benefi-

cial in yours, however, especially if you're patient enough to ask a second person to help you cart the tunnel around.

Speaking of my tendency to handle our caterpillar tunnels far too roughly, I've broken the corners apart a couple of times. To make up for my mistreatment, Mark added brackets to the inside corners to help keep the frame together. If you're like me and have no intention of being gentle with your tunnels, it might be a good idea to install brackets while you're building rather than waiting for your tunnels to break.

The image above shows the cheapest option, but we've found that small shelf brackets (like the one shown below) work even better if you're willing to pay double the cost.

Version 2.0

Mark is currently experimenting with new innovations in Version 2.0 of his caterpillar tunnels. One change is in the way he attached the insect barrier. He rolled up the fabric just like before, but this time he attached it to the top of the frame with lag screws, no strapping required. During construction, we both preferred this over the method we used in Version 1.0 of the tunnels, but over time more moths do get in through the fabric. I suspect wrapping the fabric around and attaching it to the inside of the frame would be an even better solution.

Mark is also trying to make the tunnels lighter, and to that end he's using different materials. First, he actually made half of the bottom frame heavier, upgrading from 2x3s to 2x4s on two sides for the sake of longevity. But then he finished out the long sides of the bottom frame with drop-ceiling support metal, a very light material intended for hanging industrial ceiling tiles. This counteracts the extra weight of the 2x4s while continuing the rot-resistant theme. Be sure, however, to cover the holes of the metal with tape or some other material to keep out bugs.

On the top portion of the frame, Mark used 1x4s, then added in a bit of stability with a small section of scab wood in the corner. While much lighter than version 1.0, this frame does tend to buckle with age, which allows moths in.

Finally, Mark also went for smaller pipe than in Version 1.0 for the hoops, downgrading from a 1/2-inch to 1/4-inch PVC pipe. Since the top-frame wood is only one inch thick, in this version he screwed through the wood and the pipe in order to give the frame a little more stability as you can see in the image below.

Version 2.0 of the caterpillar tunnel is still slightly experimental and not quite finished, but hopefully it'll give you some ideas for other directions that you can explore in your own garden. Overall, the key elements of the tunnels are the hoops, the bottom and top frames that fit perfectly together, and the insect-barrier fabric. How you mix those elements together is up to you!

Adding Frost Protection to Your Caterpillar Tunnel

I'll end with one last great use for caterpillar tunnels — frost protection. Those of you who have read my book *The Weekend Homesteader* may recall my chapter on using quick hoops to extend the fall and spring gardening seasons. The masterful gardener Eliot Coleman came up with this idea, and it's pretty simple. First, stick short pieces of rebar in the ground on either side of your plants. Next, take a piece of PVC pipe and slide one end over the rebar on each side of the bed. If you attach frost-protection fabric on top, you'll end up with a quick hoop that's quite good at protecting cold-hardy crops through the early parts of the winter. Depending on your location and what you're planting, you might even get harvests during the entire off-season with this approach.

The main trouble with quick hoops is that they make it relatively tough to get into your beds to work on crops or harvest them. Furthermore, you have to weigh down the fabric wherever it touches the ground, and these connecting points have a tendency to freeze and tear when you try to access the interior during cold weather. Mark's caterpillar tunnels are a better solution because they're hinged, meaning that they're always easy to get into. This allows you to harvest your hard-earned crops even amidst ice and snow.

So how do you transition your caterpillar tunnels from providing only bug protection to giving you frost protection also? First, invest in some 10-foot-wide Agribon-19 row-cover fabric. Don't be swayed into thinking that thicker fabric will protect plants better in cold weather. The perfect material is a balancing act between holding in heat and allowing light through during the winter, and the Agribon-19 weight seems to be the middle ground best suited for most home gardeners.

Measure the fabric to the length of your tunnel just like you did with the insect barrier fabric. Then, if you don't mind a little slop, simply tuck the fabric all the way under the hinged side and in between the top and bottom frames on the other three sides. (If you come up with a neater way to do this, we're all ears!)

And there you have it — a frost-protected bed that's easy to get into. Now you can harvest lettuce and kale even in the face of winter frosts.

Deer-proof Garden Fence

How to Build a Deer-proof Fence

Depending on where you live, you may be faced with various types of animal competition in your garden. But there's always something big that wants to get in and eat months of growth in a single night. For us and for many other gardeners in North America, that something is the white-tailed deer.

In a later section, I'll suggest some alternative ways to keep deer at bay. But for now, believe me when I say that a fence is the best solution for most. Our deer-proof garden fence has been in action for seven seasons and we've yet to have a single deer break in.

Weed Barrier

Before starting to build your fence, please learn from our mistake — if you don't think ahead, your fence will become a wonderful reservoir for weeds! To prevent this issue, lay down a weed barrier before you start building. A kill mulch of cardboard will work here, but only if you're relentless about keeping mulch on top. Given the challenge of getting rid of established weeds along a fenceline, I instead recommend one of the fabrics sold as a long-term weed barrier (which you should also mulch on top of for longevity's sake).

The alternative (which is sadly the case in our garden) is to give up on the part of your garden right next to the fence and weedeat that zone frequently. Even then, vines like Japanese honeysuckle are likely to get a foothold and take over. At this point, the only solution is to spray herbicides (not recommended) or move your growing space further away from the fence edge.

Framing Up Your Fence

Cautionary tale aside, let's talk construction. The gate is a great place to start since it's the most complex part of the fence. First, frame up a doorway using 4x4s sunk into the ground and cemented in place. Another 4x4 at the top serves as a brace to keep the posts from leaning in. Adding in a tensioner prevents the posts from leaning out.

Unless you have three sets of hands, attaching the overhead 4x4 involves first holding it in place with brackets, then drilling a pilot hole through each upright. Finally, hammer a 10-inch nail through each pilot hole (at which point you can remove the brackets to use somewhere else).

Next, hang a gate onto one of the uprights. We started with a simple garden gate (also known as a pasture gate), and that will be fine for many people. It's also pretty easy to install, which is a plus. For us, however, raccoons started coming in through the gap in the top, so we added some boards to stop that from happening. The result isn't as elegant but is much more functional.

After you have the gate in place, it's time to consider the corners. These are the hardest parts of the fence to do well and also the most important for structural integrity. Don't underbuild your corners!

The photo below shows the optimal corner arrangement — three upright posts in a V shape with two horizontal braces between them.

Next, install tensioners on wires that go along two diagonals overlapping the braces. Of course, all three upright 4x4s are sunk into the ground and cemented into place. The result is a very sturdy corner that will hold up over time.

If cement feels like too much work, a new product, sold as fence-post foam, is much easier to install. We first saw this chemical being used to shore up a nearby telephone pole. It foams up then solidifies, doing the job of concrete without the danger to your back from hefting heavy bags.

To install, follow the instructions for whatever brand you buy since each product will be a little different. Additionally, be aware that although fence-post foam is ten times easier to handle, in our experience it isn't quite as sturdy as concrete and is considerably more expensive.

 Another energy-saving option to consider when building your fence is automating the hole-digging portion of the project. We ended up renting a two-person auger with a 6-inch bit for half a day, which was long enough to get all of our holes bored (but was still really hard work in our heavy clay!). Another option is to hire someone with a tractor and auger attachment to do the job for you. If you're willing to spend some money to save yourself effort, this is definitely the one part of the fence most worth outsourcing.

Okay, so you now have corners and the area around your gate installed.

What's next? I hope you haven't returned your auger yet, because we recommend putting in at least a few 4x4s along the sides of each fenceline as well. These don't have to be cemented into place — simply tamping the soil back down with a spud bar at intervals while backfilling with soil will suffice.

To save energy and money, you can also use metal T-posts between the wooden posts. These are pounded into place with a post driver. Be sure to keep your fenceline straight as you install these intervening supports — a piece of twine strung between the corners will keep you on track.

Before we move on from the supports, I want to add in the potential for expansion. Despite reading that deer can jump up to ten feet, lumber constraints mean our fence only reaches eight feet high (with wire up to six feet over most of the fenceline). We'd planned to slide PVC pipes over the T-posts to add attachment points for an even higher level of wire, but this didn't turn out to be necessary in our garden. If it is in yours, the PVC pipes are our recommendation for increasing height.

Adding the Fence Material

Now that you have posts going all the way around your garden, all you need to do is attach fencing material to that frame. There are plenty of options at your local hardware store, each of which comes with pros and cons. I don't recommend plastic here since it will break down in the sun. Chicken wire also tends to have low longevity, so we went for the next grade up and used mesh-metal fencing.

It's easier to install a 4-foot roll plus a 2-foot roll than a single 6-foot roll, so that's what we did. To prevent the two spans from gaping apart, we then wove both sections of fencing together with the same wire that had been holding the roll shut.

A fence like ours is excellent at keeping out deer, but we learned the hard way that it's not rabbit-proof, squirrel-proof, or chipmunk-proof. We'll talk about dealing with those problems later in this book. If you're willing to invest considerably more in your fencing material, though, you can keep even small critters out at the fence level. In addition to choosing fencing with small holes, you'll want to dig a trench and extend the fencing material at least a few inches into the soil.

So there you go! This fence requires a moderate amount of money and energy, but it will definitely save you enough heartache to make it worthwhile in the long run. Say goodbye to deer eating your crops and say hello to delicious returns for your hard work!

Other Ways to Deter Deer

If the cost or time commitment of building a fence is excessive, or if a fence simply won't work for you and your garden, there *are* other options you can try to keep deer away. I'll include a quick rundown here, but please keep in mind that after gardening for nearly two decades, our biggest regret is that we didn't build a deer-proof fence sooner.

You've likely seen all the products on the market being billed as a quick fix to the deer problem, or maybe you've seen social media posts touting the wonders of deer-repellent plants. The unfortunate truth is that none of these deterrents really work unless your deer pressure is very low. Believe me, we've given almost everything out there a whirl.

The only semi-effective method is tossing plastic fence material over your yummiest plants, like sweet potatoes and strawberries. But even this is just a stopgap measure and not a permanent solution. (It will, how- ever, deter goats if you like to take them out to graze on the cover crops during the off-season ... as long as your eye remains on your caprine friends.)

When we lived in Virginia, half a mile from the nearest road and a mile from our nearest neighbor, we did come up with a cheap and mostly effective permaculture alternative. It had four parts, and totally wouldn't work where we live now. But I'm going to give you a rundown just in case you're in the backwoods or want to take inspiration from some of these layered solutions.

Part one was Lucy, our amazing dog. She spent a lot of time patrolling the perimeter, but despite her hard work, deer still sometimes got in.

Part two was to build chicken moats. A chicken moat involves two 4-foot-tall fences spaced relatively close together. A deer could jump over one of the fences pretty easily, but they feel less safe if stuck in the

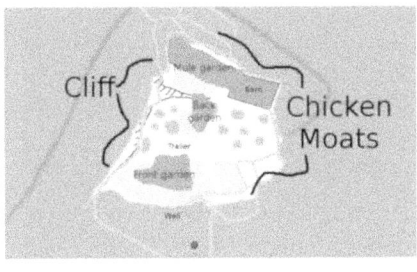

middle of two barriers. The area between the fences is maintained as pasture for chickens, making it worth the expense of building such sprawling fencelines.

Part three, detailed on the website backyarddeer.com, was an invention of Mark's. In essence, it's a motorized deer scarer based on a drill, a golf ball, and a piece of flashing. Every time the scarer banged, deer who had snuck past Lucy and through the deer moats took off.

Part four was a gun and a freezer. We ended up killing and eating several deer who'd eaten our crops. (Yes, you do need to apply for a kill permit to hunt deer on your own land during the off-season.)

Obviously, these techniques won't work in most locations. A typical home is too close to roads for dogs to run free unsupervised. A gun can be a hazard on a small property even if your stomach is strong enough to let you butcher the resulting meat. And my guess is that your neighbors wouldn't be too thrilled about the perpetual clanging coming from a scarer either.

All in all, if you want to keep deer from using your garden as their personal pantry, you really should build a fence.

Critter-proof Strawberry Beds

The Sad Story of Our Ohio Strawberries

The history of our garden is chock-full of sad stories with happy endings, and usually that happy ending involves Mark saving the day. This particular story is built around strawberries, a fruit which I absolutely adore. After our move to Ohio, however, this became a problem.

Back when we lived in Virginia, we had a great strawberry patch. It provided all the fresh fruit even I could eat, which is saying something. So when we relocated, we brought some of the plants with us and were ready for similar success. I set out a patch and the plants grew really well during their first season.

With strawberries, you pick off any flowers that appear in their initial year of growing, preparing the plants for producing fruits starting in the second season. So when the next year rolled around and my plants bloomed, I started anticipating the delicious flavor of our first Ohio strawberries.

Enter this story's villains — chipmunks! The adorable but pesky rodents slipped through our fence and picked every single berry before there was even a hint of red visible. To add insult to injury, the chipmunks didn't even eat the bounty they picked. Instead, they dragged the  fruits across the garden and dropped them in random places as if to say, "This is what you would have eaten if I wasn't here."

Over the course of multiple years, I spent a lot of time and effort trying to figure out ways to keep the strawberries away from the chipmunks. Nothing worked. Eventually, I just ripped the strawberry plants out. It felt like there was no point putting so much energy into the patch without getting any harvest back.

When Mark saw what was happening, he said, "Anna. No. We're not giving up on strawberries. I can fix this!"

So he built the strawberry planters I'll describe in this chapter. I bought new plants, put them in, and babied them. But I didn't think the effort was going to pay off. I'd tried so many options already.

Well, I'm here to say that Mark was right and I was wrong. We're now eating delicious homegrown strawberries, and there's lots more to come.

In the next section, I'll show you how to build a strawberry planter that keeps the chipmunks out but still lets pollinators and rain and everything else your plants need in. An easy fix to a gnarly problem!

How to Build a Critter-proof Strawberry Bed

The strawberry planter is essentially a raised bed with a hinged cover. As you might expect for such a project, the first step is to choose lumber (treated decking boards), then to build the frame.

Other than the type of wood used, these are similar to the frames we made for the anti-caterpillar tunnels — one rectangle on top of another rectangle. Eight-foot long sides will maximize lumber use. Then you can choose to either maximize lumber again with four-foot short sides, or to focus on ease of management with three-foot short sides.

Either way, with the frames completed it's time to start thinking of anti-critter measures. Underneath the bottom rectangle, Mark attached a layer of hardware cloth so chipmunks don't dig up from underground. While I'm not sure that this was an entirely necessary addition to the bed, it's much better to be safe than sorry!

I filled the bottom rectangle with manure and old potting soil. (See the Porch Planter Boxes chapter for a rundown on other options for soil alternatives.) Since plant roots can grow through the hardware cloth into the surrounding soil, it's not actually imperative that you use something other than plain old dirt to fill the planter box. But good soil does make for happy plants.

Next, Mark added two door hinges to attach the top and bottom wooden frames together. Then all that's left is to ensure that the chipmunks can't hop in from the top.

To that end, Mark stretched plastic mesh across the upper frame, choosing a product with holes small enough to keep chipmunks out while pollinators and rain easily pass through. He attached the plastic using a combination of exterior screws with small washers, which keeps the mesh firmly affixed to the structure.

And that's all there is to it! Given how high our strawberry bill would be without a homegrown alternative, we figure the bed will pay for itself in a couple of years.

Recipe: Mixed-Berry Fool

Ingredients:

- Fresh strawberries from your garden or from a farmer's market. (Store-bought strawberries don't work as well.)

- Assorted other berries. (You don't need other berries, but you can include any you have on hand, up to the same amount of strawberries you used.)

- Sugar

- Whipped cream (optional)

Directions:

1. Cut off the stems of your strawberries and slice them into small pieces.

2. Sprinkle enough sugar onto your strawberries to lightly coat all surfaces. Mix well.

3. Let soak for half an hour, allowing the sugar to pull the juices out of the berries.

4. Add in the other berries and mix.

5. If you like, garnish with whipped cream.

6. Enjoy!

(Anti-)Bird Netting

As a berry lover, another problem I faced is birds getting to my bushes and picking the fruits before I could. I came to Mark with my problem, and he said, "No problem, I can fix that." Sure enough, he did!

The result is an anti-bird netting system that keeps cardinals and other winged predators out of the garden. It's not very expensive or time-consuming to create, although we do have one problem with our system (more on that below).

∞

How to Build an Anti-Bird Netting Enclosure

The anti-bird netting enclosure is simple to install. The only major mistake we made was not putting down a weed barrier around the fence line before beginning. **Do this first!** Otherwise, you'll end up with vines growing up through your berry netting, making the entire thing very difficult to manage.

That warning aside, start by purchasing plastic berry netting, which is pretty cheap stuff if you buy it in small widths. We sprang for 7.5-foot width netting, at a cost of around 40 bucks for our entire enclosure (top and sides).

Of course, a 7.5-foot width isn't going to be enough to cover much berry at all. So for the top, we took some rope and wove it along the edges of two different widths of berry netting, in and out all the way down to the end of our enclosure. This attaches pieces together, meaning that you can create any width of netting you choose to.

For length, make sure you span the entire top of your berry enclosure then add a foot or two on each side. You can always cut a too-long berry ceiling shorter, but making it longer is a bear. Err on the side of too much!

To hold the netting top up, you'll need to add connecting points onto your fence — eye bolts are a good choice here. Your rope then ties into clips and/or turnbuckles so the top is easy to put up and take down annually.

We used a turnbuckle on one side to allow tensioning (see above) and a clip on the other side for simplicity (see below).

Now you're ready to add berry netting to the sides, which is simple if you're working with an existing fence. Just stretch the netting across the fence wire then use rope or whatever you have on hand to weave it into place the same way you connected ceiling widths together.

Finally, clip the dangling ends of the top netting to the sides using clothespins. Wooden pins will work, but stainless steel clothespins stand up to the elements best over the long run.

While this anti-bird enclosure does its job well, the top *does* tend to sag over long expanses of netting. In order to solve that problem, you'll want to add some center supports made of U-posts and PVC pipes to the enclosure that keep the ceiling high enough.

I recommend short U-posts, as small as you can get them, combined with long PVC pipes (six feet or more high). If I'd planned these inner supports during the initial build, I would have gone higher with the pipes. But as it was, I cut the PVC pipes as long as I could without putting undue stress on the berry netting and risking a tear.

Old flower pots on top of the pipes prevent holes from being poked in the berry netting. Anything smooth would work up there — consider cut-down milk jugs or cottage-cheese containers. (If you do tear a hole, you can fix it using the rope-weaving method mentioned above.)

As for post spacing, I don't have a tried-and-true rule here. The posts are easy to move around, though, so you can play with them to decide what makes sense for your patch. Or you could build more permanent inner supports with lumber. Either way, your hats and hairdos will definitely be glad you dealt with the sag.

Taking the Netting Down for the Winter

Each year after berry season is over, you should take your netting down for the winter. While you *can* get away with leaving it up (we did one year due to illness), there will definitely be damage due to fallen leaves and snow. Rather than setting aside an hour in the spring for repairs, why not take fifteen minutes to prevent problems from popping up in the first place?

First, remove the clothespins attaching the top netting to the sides. Hopefully, your fence was installed with weed barriers and this will be an easy task.

Next, undo the clips on one width of the top netting at a time. Having a second person involved makes it easy to roll each width of netting over onto the next one as you work.

Keep rolling until you reach the end. We simply drop the netting burrito onto the ground for the winter, which works fine as long as you put it back up before weeds start to grow through in the spring. Similarly, if you use stainless steel clothespins those can remain outside clipped to the fence without a problem.

That's all you have to do ... other than to enjoy your delicious raspberries, blackberries, and blueberries in front of the jealous birds!

Plant Support with U-Posts

This final project is ultra-simple. In fact, it's so simple I almost didn't include it in the book.

But some of you might have building skills closer to mine than to Mark's. If everything else looks really challenging, you can start with these U-post tricks. The posts are simple to use and give your plants lots of help in the garden.

First, you'll want to select your posts. There are two main types of metal posts available in most stores. U-posts look like a "U" in cross-section. In contrast, T-posts are much heavier duty and are shaped like a "T" in the cross-section

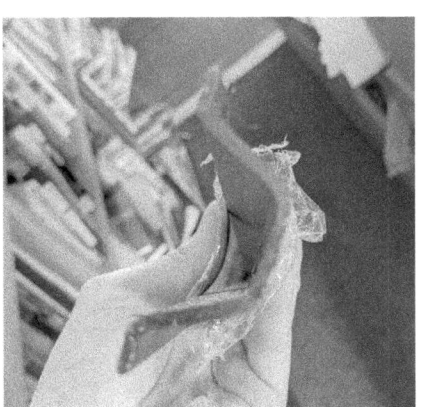

Photo credit: Duncan Wall

The reason I love U-posts is that they're really easy to put in and to take out. They have a little notch of metal near the base that can simply be stepped on to drive the bottom into soft soil. If necessary, you can also pound the post in with a mallet or a post driver.

Go easy with the hammering though — you'll need about the same amount of force to remove a U-post as you used to install it. The beauty of U-posts is that they can be moved around the garden and used for multiple purposes over the course of a single season. But only if you didn't go crazy and install them too deep in hard soil!

That said, I sometimes just leave U-posts in one location permanently. The picture above shows an example of one use that I absolutely adore involving **asparagus**.

I drove a U-post into each end of a row of the plants, then I stretched three wires between the posts (high, middle, and low). You can also use string instead of wire in this type of application.

As plants grow, I weave them between the three horizontal wires, alternating which side of each wire the plant passes by. So if a stem starts on the right side of the bottom wire, I guide it to the left of the middle wire, then to the right of the top wire. (If starting on the left, the pattern would be left-right-left instead.) This weaving pattern naturally supports the stems without needing individual ties or clips, making it easy to remove dead growth in winter.

This asparagus setup has been doing great for seven years now and I doubt I'll have to change it over the life of the plants. You can also use this type of weaving on annual crops like indeterminate tomatoes.

That said, we prefer a different setup (also using U-posts) with **tomatoes**. We train to three stems, pruning away lower leaves and excess suckers while attaching each stem to a six-foot U-post to keep them off the ground (a reservoir for blight). Small pieces of wire or twine are our choice for attachment, but a more traditional approach is to tie tomatoes up using strips torn from old sheets.

No matter how you train your tomatoes, you'll definitely want to rotate them to a different patch of garden every year. That's why U-posts are such a good fit here. It takes me about a minute to put in each tomato post and another minute to pull it out, so there's no hurdle to using the same equipment in a different spot.

Another great temporary use for U-posts is staking up **kale** and other top-heavy plants going to seed. In this application, I simply put a post on each side of the plants once they start to topple over, then use a loop of baling twine to tie the plants up. After I've collected the seeds, the arrangement can be taken down in seconds.

Finally, U-posts work perfectly in conjunction with plastic trellis material. **Peas** are what we trellis the most in this way, although we've also been known to use this technique with **cucumbers** and even **butternut squash**.

For this application, you'll need two or more U-posts to support the trellis (with the number determined by the heaviness of the plants and the length of your row). Each post comes with little hooks, the top ones facing up and the lower ones facing down. Simply slide the trellis material into these hooks, pulling tight so it won't sag and come loose. If necessarily, you can twist a bit of wire through holes in the U-post to keep the trellis material in place.

Similarly, you can make basic tree tubes to protect saplings from chickens scratching and deers browsing using a single U-post and a piece of trellis material wrapped into a cylinder. Don't expect these to hold up against serious grazing pressure, but they can be enough to set young trees in wild areas off to a good start.

Ultimately, U-posts are a really handy support to have in your garden. They're easy to install, easy to take down, and the green ones blend in well with your crops. I highly recommend investing in some if you haven't already!

Choose a Project, Go Out, and DIY!

If your head is spinning as you try to figure out which project to work on first, I've got one tip for you: Choose whichever one makes you smile...or whichever one you think you can finish before your spouse gets sick and tired of you lollygagging and sneaks into your work area to steal your hammer in the night.

And once you've finished all those projects, I hope you'll check out our Udemy course, "Soil-First Gardening: How to Grow Black Gold in the Backyard." The videos include lots of ways to improve your garden from the ground up, including two DIY hacks that you might enjoy. One involves turning a rolling garbage bin into a black-soldier-fly colony, and the other takes an old bathtub and uses it to raise compost worms.

Of course, our other books are also chock-full of DIY projects. *$10 Root Cellar* offers guidelines to create exactly what the title says, while *Trailersteading* helps you turn a low-cost mobile home into the center of a homestead.

The other thing you can do is to sign up for our email list for monthly tips (and a free book!) at wetknee.com/free-books. Mark is constantly coming up with new ways to solve my problems, and his innovations may solve yours too.

Looking forward to seeing you over there, and thanks for making us a part of your gardening journey!

Appendix: Supply List

Porch Planter Box

Every porch or deck is different, and how yours is set up will impact your required supplies. Here's a starter list that you can tweak to your exact specifications.

- 2x4s: Number and length will depend on how high and long you want your box to be.

- 4x4s: These are great for extra stability on the corners. Plan to cut each 4x4 into sections to match the height of your box.

- Brackets: These are used to attach wood to your porch surface. Three brackets we used in construction of our porch planter box are 4x4 brackets, 2x4 brackets, and (a budget option) shelf brackets.

- Plywood to use for the walls: The cheapest kind of plywood works, but do not use particle board!

- Exterior screws

- Paint: The more coats of paint on your inner walls, the longer the plywood will last. Exterior paint is best, and the type rated for barns tends to be inexpensive.

- Vinyl siding: This isn't required, but it does make the outside of your planter box prettier.

- If you're adding on the extra shelf, you'll need 2x8s (at whatever length you want your shelf to be) and heavy duty L brackets.

- Potting soil and/or manure: If you're buying bagged potting soil, our favorite brand is Happy Frog,

- Clear corrugated roofing material: You'll want to purchase this locally. Be sure to put the UV-resistant side up. (Optional: only necessary if your roof is angled so water runs off into your planter box.)

- Plastic netting for trellises (If you're going to build a berry enclosure, you're likely to have some scraps left for trellising.)

- Row-cover fabric for season extension: You might have scraps leftover from your (Anti-)Caterpillar Tunnel project. If not, we recommend growbiggerplants brand Agribon AG-19 Floating Row Cover.

(Anti-)Caterpillar Tunnel

We've included a supply list for the tried-and-true version 1.0 below plus some notes on the experimental version 2.0.

Version 1.0:

◦ Treated 2x3s or 2x4s: While you can make large caterpillar tunnels using six 2x4s (one on each long side, top and bottom, and one cut in half to make the ends, again doubled for top and bottom), we eventually decided that this size is too heavy and tends to become damaged when moved by a single person. Our preferred size now uses four 2x4s and clocks in at four feet on each side. Be sure to choose treated wood for longevity. 2X3s also work, but tend to rot faster.

◦ Exterior screws

◦ Two door hinges per tunnel

◦ Eight brackets per tunnel

◦ PVC pipes: The goal is to make half circle ribs to hold up your Agribon material. You'll need five for an 8-foot length or three for a 4-foot length. We originally used the same pipes we had for our quick hoops, but 1/2-inch PVC is probably overkill in this application. You could get away with a narrower width or could experiment with the easier-to-cut PEX tubing we used in version 2.0.

◦ One furring strip: Either four feet or eight feet long, depending on the length of your tunnel.

◦ Two small pieces of flexible wire: Scraps will work fine here.

◦ Paint to cover the wood: The more coats, the longer your lumber will last. Exterior paint is best, and the type rated for barns tends to be inexpensive.

◦ Ag-Fabric Garden Netting: There are some cheaper versions out there, but I recommend going for the tried-and-true since lesser brands break down in the sun very quickly. This one has lasted for four years so far.

◦ ¾-inch self-drilling Lath screws to attach your insect netting to the upper rectangle.

◦ Plastic strapping. This is used to keep the lid from hitting plants in the next row when open. If you don't have strapping on hand but do have rope, that will work just as well (although it may be harder to attach to your frame).

◦ 10-foot-wide Agribon-19 row-cover fabric: Don't be tempted into thinking that thicker fabric will protect plants more. It's a tradeoff between holding in heat and allowing light through, and the Agribon-19 weight seems to be the perfect middle ground for most home gardeners. We buy ours from Johnny's in big rolls, but Amazon also has shorter sections for less exuberant gardeners available in an off-brand.

◦ An experiment we haven't done yet but are considering for version 3.0: Putting some type of firm, thin plastic on the bottom of the treated 2x4s for added protection where the wood touches the ground. A piece of vinyl siding cut to fit would work.

Version 2.0:

Same supplies as above, but using different materials for the frame:

◦ One treated 2x4.

◦ Drop ceiling grid main beam 144-inch galvanized steel: These were available at Lowes for $11.45 each at the time of publication. Cutting one section in half provides both long sections of your bottom rectangle.

° Duct tape: To cover up the holes in the metal sections.

° 1x4s: Three eight-foot boards can be cut to build your upper rectangle. However, our wood did tend to warp away from the metal frame after a year or so using boards this thin. Perhaps try a thicker size?

° One roll of PEX tubing, either ½-inch or 1-inch depending on how high you need your tunnel to be. (Wider tubing has the structural ability to span a longer distance and to allow taller plants underneath.)

Deer-proof Garden Fence

- Weed-barrier fabric: We're currently experimenting with Hoople brand four-foot weed barrier. A four-foot width, however, might not be quite enough if your weeds are exuberant.

- Maybe some landscaping blocks on top of the weed barrier if you can afford it. Mulch if you can't. Either way, be sure to spend extra time and money on the weed barrier to save lots of trouble in the future!

- Treated 4x4's to form the perimeter of your fence: Plan on five for each corner and three to frame up the gate. For longer fence spans, you'll be happier if you include 4x4s at intervals within each side as well.

- T-posts to support the fence in between the 4x4s.

- Tensioners and wire for the gate and corners

- Bracket to temporarily hold up the support 4x4s

- Galvanized, welded-wire fencing material sufficient to wrap all the way your garden as many times as necessary to reach the desired height. (We recommend aiming for a six-foot height.) You can get these from Amazon, but you're likely to get this much cheaper at your local hardware store. When choosing hole size, there's a major tradeoff in price and utility; the smallest holes will keep out the most critters but will also cost the most.

- Bags of Quickrete to secure your 4x4 posts. (Plan on half a bag per post at a minimum.)

- If you want to try foam, one option is Fast 2K b. (Don't use this at the corners or around your gate!)

- Fasteners to attach your fence to the posts: Fencing staples are cheap at your local hardware store, but fancier options, such as the Cat's Claw Fasteners brand, are also available from Amazon.

- Farm gate with hinge hardware.

- 9-inch galvanized nails to help make your 4x4 corner braces.

Critter-proof Strawberry Bed

- Six treated 8-foot decking boards per bed (two of which will be cut into 4-foot lengths to make the short sides).

- Two door hinges

- Hardware cloth to protect the top and bottom. Vinyl-coated cloth is just a little more money but boasts a longer life span. Alternatively, semi-rigid plastic trellis material with small holes will also work great here. For the top, make sure the holes are large enough for bees to fly through to allow pollination.

- Exterior screws

- Washers to go around the screws when securing the hardware cloth/trellis material

- Galvanized handle

(Anti-)Bird netting

- Rolls of bird netting, with the amount you use depending on how much area you're protecting. (Keep in mind the fact that you need to make walls as well as a ceiling and plan for a one- or two-foot overlap of material between the two.)

- Rope to weave multiple sections of bird netting together.

- Eye bolts

- Turnbuckles with an eye bolt on one end and a hook on the other

- Clip

- Stainless steel clothespins to connect the bird netting together

- 3-foot U-posts: You can get these on Amazon, but you're really better off buying them locally.

- 1.5-inch PVC pipes to slide over U-posts.

- Flower pots, yogurt containers, or other items to sit on top of the U-posts.

Plant Support with U-Posts

- I like having various sizes of U-posts on hand, but my favorites are 4-foot and 6-foot lengths.

- Plastic trellis material: My favorite kind is the same stuff that's used as caution fencing in construction zones (only green instead of orange)

- Steel galvanized wire

Index

www.ingramcontent.com/pod-product-compliance
Ingram Content Group UK Ltd.
Pitfield, Milton Keynes, MK11 3LW, UK
UKHW040746060225
454761UK00001B/118